CW01651002

THE CONFESSIONS

Christopher DeWeese

~

Periplum Open Book Competition Winner

Periplum
Poetry

Published by PERIPLUM
2017
First edition

Series Editor: Anthony Caleshu
Periplum is published out of the
Department of English and Creative Writing
Plymouth University
School of Humanities
6 Portland Villas
Plymouth PL4 8AA
UK

To purchase Periplum titles,
or to enter our annual book competition, please visit:
www.plymouth.ac.uk/periplum
email: periplum@plymouth.ac.uk

ISBN: 978-0-9935391-3-8
Design & typeset by Dean Owens

Contents

I was a diving bell / 6
I was a panharmonic singing bird / 8
I was the first twenty-one gun salute / 10
I was a phantasmagoria / 12
I was a curiosity / 14
I was a regulation dueling field / 16
I was a garden maze / 18
I was a celebrity jumper / 20
I was twisted inside a tiny cabinet / 22
I was a gentleman botanist / 24
I was a wagon train / 26
I was a street chaunter / 28
I was a lightning rod salesman / 30
I was a spirit photographer / 32
I was a company town / 34
I was an optimistic linguist / 36
I was a sheet music tycoon / 38
I was a medicine show / 40
I was a polar explorer / 42
I was the greatest art potter / 44
I was the first steel-wire suspension bridge / 46
I was a pickle barrel modified to infamy / 48
I was a living insignia / 50
I was an aristocratic detective/ 52
I was a traditional convict / 54
I was a builder of champions / 56
I was encased in a block of ice / 58
I was a drift of wrecked sailors / 60

I was a revolutionary artist / 62
I was two anarchist bullfighters / 64
I was a forger's apprentice / 66
I was a wartime censor / 68
I was a lonely heiress / 70
I was an airborne crew / 72
I was a professional spy / 74
I was a flea tamer / 76
I was ghostmaster / 78
I was an alcoholic mascot / 80
I was a stage magician / 82
I was the legendary singing moose of Calgary / 84
I was an auctioneering champion / 86
I was a handsome privateer / 88
I was a second-tier airport chaplain / 90
I was a home for old soldiers / 92
I was a cliff-side lookout / 94
I was a performing bear impersonator / 96
I was a modernist cemetery / 98
I was a bankrupt circus / 100
I was a county fairground / 102
I was an invisible man / 104

For Dara

I was a diving bell

I was a diving bell
salvaging cannon from a warship sunk deep

where the sea stopped
to grow its famous beards
and braid them into gowns.

A furious salutation erupted
as I descended.

The divers inside me
thought of nothing for ballast
but death.

Our trajectory curved slightly,
a plumb line
the fathoms diminished.

The waves looked suspicious
licking their migrations and then retreating,
theirs a sinking
both strategic and understated.

Our King was far away,
but his fingerprints remained.

Metal, afraid, I slowly raised them.

I was a panharmonic singing bird

I was a panharmonic singing bird
with detachable wings
and the carefully gilded larynx
of a deceased soprano

who willed her personality
"and all that implies" to extravagance,
a gold snuff-box enclosing us.

My calcified feathers
and tropical pince-nez
harmonized courteously
toward some aesthetic dream of permanence.

Strings and weights
replaced my ventricles
with stricter motives, beveled edges.

To approximate the luxurious eyebrows
great conductors lasso
to pull soulful machines
from their orchestras,

some wizard hid gears
between my lacquered skin
and this fancy breath
peasants thought miraculous

before they guillotined everything.

I was the first twenty-one gun salute

I was the first twenty-one gun salute
a republic received from a monarch,

one fort ashore
and another at sea
rendering an arsenal of honors so formally

even the gulls stopped,
white rocks streaking.

The silence that I preceded
was renowned for its distance,

clouds lowering their sails
as gunpowder fell
to mascara.

Custom raised the waves' white flags.
It was Christmas.

Ruffles and flourishes echoed their militant attentions
as short timing chants
filled the incidental peripheries
conscripts know well.

If I wasn't a sailor, I'd be a bird.
If I wasn't a soldier, I'd have a drink.

Gun for gun, I beat.

I was a phantasmagoria

I was a phantasmagoria,
a pandemonium of opaque ghosts
filling abandoned crypts
in a winning general

of whom there existed
no standard likeness
but a bulbous nose
and a well-known missing appendage.

A foto-player with levers for thunder
and funeral bells
led the rumble, chanting
We are Here but Not Here.

My illusions shivered,
their afterworld cold and traditional.

Against what smoke
a coffin could be rigged to blow,
the screams I conscripted
transcended all those hitherto attempted,

walls and chains giving way
to a terror so native

that inside our skin
its nails lay waiting.

I was a curiosity

I was a curiosity
after I died

because my body turned to soap,
my nails kept growing,
and I wrote these poems

between a cemetery
subsequent Philadelphias would deny existed
and the yellow ropes
that surrounded my exhibit.

Certain businessmen found me a port
in the inclement weather
of their own personal tragedies.

Supply, they whispered,
trying to explain why
their fingers turned to knives
they rubbed against me,

hoping wrongly that I cared
to bless their wretched, consumptive lives.

One thing is certain:
eight straight pins and two four-hole buttons
were stuck within my stomach.
Everything else seems dubious.

Did I sculpt pretend animals
then eat them?

Did I fuck with the wrong magician?

I was a regulation dueling field

I was a regulation dueling field.

It was always dawn,
the horizon melodramatically trying on ghosts
of the men who stood beneath

like bottled smoke,
ready to release one quick pose
before disappearing completely.

The sky never challenged anyone
so much as it encouraged them
to accidentally shoot it
full of nightly animals.

For me, inspiration was a sound.
The moment before one man falls.

The seconds embraced
their own obscurity,
elaborately mustached
as if even their mouths were understudies.

To ready the italic pistols,
they whispered the Russian word for winter
into each barrel.

I was a garden maze

I was a garden maze,
an anxious geometry
of dead-ends and topiary

intercepting formal space
to create a sudden, floral privacy.

Lost, peasants left themselves
inside my reaches,
yelling little fires between the green horses
and disproportionate swans I kept.

After a few days,
they ploughed homesteads.

In this way, my veins became full of dancing.

Balloonists saw what I couldn't,
paths strewn like the scattered pages
of an etiquette book

left to instruct my descendants
in all the most important things,

like how to eat fish with a general,
how you impersonate a window.

I was a celebrity jumper

I was a celebrity jumper
plummeting so fast
that my falling turned the crowd around me
to just one gasp:

first an onrushing admirer,
and then a terrible silence
until I burst triumphant
from the cruel, jagged waters.

To test the wind,
I threw a bear cub in ahead of me.

To test my nation's heart,
I kissed its flag.
I dedicated every stunt to my mother.

In fragrant saloons,
a fraternity of laborers bet on nothing less
than the rigid particulars
of my own death.

I held their wagers beneath my tongue
every time I leapt.

I was twisted inside a tiny cabinet

I was twisted inside a tiny cabinet
and obscured by a waterfall
of useless machinery,

oh yes I was hardly breathing
within the technology I motored,

a garish automaton
known across the continent
for its exotic dress
and prodigious chess playing ability.

To move a marionette from underneath,
it is like performing a ghost dance.

You rattle chains
to cover up your sneezing.

Your form leaks
so far as the dim light carries,
a flickering, dirty shadow.

Chess was everything to me,
an anonymous factory
whose product was its strategy.

In the darkness
of my own authoring,
I imagined a whole world
of men disguised as machines.

The pedal-rigged clouds.
The sympathetic trees.

I was a gentleman botanist

I was a gentleman botanist
translating the jungle into Latinate,

handsome as a flag
painted on an egg

as gumboots danced their own safaris
far away.

When my sickness came,
it stayed campfire thick in me.

The birds started speaking
and suddenly I understood captivity,
the distance between species,
the monsters cartographers invent
to fill unknown space.

Green, I fell beside you.

I shall praise your mandibles first,
and then your creeper-vines,
your casual indifference
to the body's theoretical spirit.

Above us, the sky became an astrology
more feast than animal,
a local delicacy that turns out to be
eating your own mouth.

I was a wagon train

I was a wagon train
lost between persecutions
and a better west,

where gold was said to be
the antecedent of local weather

and sourdough trees
fell themselves into Yankee cabins
wherever a bed was needed.

Nothing but California or native arrows
could fill my eyes

as I slept, nestled between the pump organ
and the godless land
to whom I offered my steps,

that endless highway
of lonely pasture.

Wheels divided the plains into pie charts
when I crouched,
dowsing for signs of my enemies.

Thunder usually meant bad tidings,
as did any weather.

Wildflowers shattered
where my children stumbled
under their giant bibles.

I was a street chaunter

I was a street chaunter
yelling libelous broadsides endlessly,

a hundred dumb little ditties
that stocked gossip with handsome flesh,
additional sailors, and "signature wigs"

through the England
of the England of the Sonnets.

At park entrances,
I sold love garlands and penny merriments,

my diversions undershooting heeled gents
and their pale brides
for the vanity of the lower orders,

who didn't mind
trading sense for rhyme.

A soft, behaved rain
slept against the legible windows.

The gaslights dimmed
as if making a conscious decision
to haunt their own neighborhoods.

A stage appeared
where my mouth should have been.

I was a lightning rod salesman

I was a lightning rod salesman
preaching copper
past the imaginary hills

settlers construct
to forsake every direction but dirt.

My handshake was a bird,
all getaway
by the time knife fights traced
the sky's nightly veins.

Between the grave of a man
persecuted for wearing his beard
and a well-governed Florida,

the thunder repeated itself
like a prizefighter who couldn't bear to leave
a clean stage.

Would you prefer a wife
or a heap of charred offal?
I reasoned with the terrible farmers.

To demonstrate what might happen,
I tried on shivers.

To stand for the sky's jagged flesh,
my hands turned to rain.

I was a spirit photographer

I was a spirit photographer
in the vague little industry of selling ghosts,

smudging faces above each portrait
until they looked strange enough
to seem irrefutable

then mumbling to evade suspicion,
my mouth a glass plate
fogged in trick negatives.

I framed evocations,
their white hands pointing
dramatically as poems set to music

toward where I stood,
fraudulent and sort of religious.

When the magistrate came,
I confessed immediately.

Yes, I was guilty
of spectacular, unprecedented conjures,
daguerreotyping flowers to society brains.

No, I did not traverse that life so indigent
we barely share its alphabet,

those glowing faces
when I closed my eyes.

I was a company town

I was a company town,
a modest house of debtors

tucked between the unmade mountains
and blinding wildflowers
the dumb, quiet West surrendered
like a thousand birds to be named later.

I rolled up my sleeves
and recruited the forest,
whose citizens hid
their spirit technologies inside local fires,

little cloud factories
eroding the moss-bit distances.

My heart was a dormitory of tiny workers
and their gold-plated forks.

All night, they sang the lullabies
I sold them like a quiet lottery,
and I felt efficient,

like a man eating a fish
just to teach him something.

I was an optimistic linguist

I was an optimistic linguist
constructing an international auxiliary language
to foster mutual aid and understanding

through the anguished forests
and quarrelsome districts
of a world broken into irregular speeches.

I thought grown-ups were omnipotent,
so I grew up whispering.

Certain I could destroy
all the world's evils,

I hammered a simple, plastic tongue
of regular junctions
and well-tuned vowels.

The language of spies,
the regime proclaimed me,
burning not only the dictionaries
but the lungs that held me

waiting beneath the everywhere
like some root
to be song.

I was a sheet music tycoon

I was a sheet music tycoon
tuning contemporary tragedies
into a balladry
families could gather around.

My real estate was in music:
a scorched zeppelin,
a railroad collision,
a tree full of violinists.

All the bravest orphans
worked for me.

They lurched through my office,
skinny voices filling the distance
in tin-pan madrigals.

Even the letters wept
over each cover

as if their promises of nostalgic shipwrecks
had already been delivered,

pianos full of wildfires and kidnapped twins
filling my nation's parlors
in hasty, moral scenes
and familiar melodies.

I was a medicine show

I was a medicine show
fumbling through the dust-grounds
summer underwrote

with assistance from Wizard Oil,
distributors of amazing tonics
foul-tasting enough to seem miraculous

Goodnight, Georgia,
or whoever you were, wherever I was.

As I slept, you whispered laws
I thought were rhetorical questions,
your pies a delicious breath
following me.

Goodnight, Texas.

The fake elixirs I sold
glowed like lava that never hardens
because it's amazing.

The yokel moon
and all the widows who believed in it
swooned like pigeons,

totally gypsy and swooning
as the night went snakeskin
and I lied, again, amazingly.

I was a polar explorer

I was a polar explorer
using my interior beard
and frozen shadow

to paddle away
from that long monogram
whose womb birthed the ice.

Swallows broke as the waves unfroze.

Clouds lowered their own grayscale,
turning the entire continent
to accommodate new visitors

until the stars gave something back,
a reckoning that relented
into a slow, human season.

A crevasse held my companions.
They died every time
I thought of them.

I, who had smoked my own whiskers,
whittled hardtack into a new hand,
that at least my silhouette
might salute correctly

should our Queen wish
to claim her new and useless land.

I was the greatest art potter

I was the greatest art potter
but only I knew it,
photographing myself holding signs that read
Unequaled, Unrivaled, and Undisputed

before burying my work
in the natural museum of history,
a grave I folded
between the 1890s and obscurity.

Shapes came to me
as verses to the prophet,
but I couldn't eat what I made in pottery.

The functional world collapsed
into an architecture of folds.

I cast my babies,
coated them in strange electric glazes.

A thousand things went democrat:
mostly tragic fires,
but also the decorative mode,
which conspired to prove inadequate
my world of hands.

I dressed up as Father Time
and pointed abroad.

I closed my eyes,
tied my mustache in a knot.

I was the first steel-wire suspension bridge

I was the first steel-wire suspension bridge,
a colossal feat of engineering

all harped up
in the dumbstruck air
where balloonists cast fireworks
and gunships feted industry

then left me slow and broad
for citizens to cross between.

Twenty-one elephants paraded
to prove my stability

a year after opening week,
when a sudden crowd
had decided I was about to sink
and stampeded,

sun-down in the tyrant wind,
the rhythmic sick of calamity.

In order to fund my completion,
the city stored wine in my anchorages,
where the temperature was constant,
the walls full of dark-lit doggerel.

He who loveth not wine, women and song,
he remaineth a fool his whole life long.

Settled in the sediment
as the flood-tide surrounded me
I hummed along.

I was a pickle barrel modified to infamy

I was a pickle barrel modified to infamy
seventeen minutes past
achieving the Falls,

that impossible feat,
the paragon of devilry itself

bested by a destitute
in a feathered hat
as flashbulbs shot asterisks
like flowers across my path.

A Beautiful Death The Hard Way,
the tabloids had predicted,

a common pessimism
that would soon be abandoned
to sell pamphlets

on *How to Weight an Anvil for Ballast*
or *How to Stunt Without a License.*

Sunshine scratched thin tickets
from the water like bears,

something baptismal in even the fish
who waited there
to witness the bellow-hissing attendants.

A new music.
A woman inside me, alive and delirious.

I was a living insignia

I was a living insignia,
a photographic reproduction
of the president's face
arranged from twenty-thousand soldiers,

a souvenir all metaphor
just like any souvenir sold to enlisted men:

commemorative hearts,
necklaces of spent ammunition,
an autographed tourniquet.

Silence overtook the staging area
and then extended it

like the chase scene
that takes place mid-air
during a staring contest.

Trumpets completed the fixed perspective.

We are at war, the men reminded themselves,
each platoon frozen
into a jawbone, a hairline,
a famous birthmark.

We could march like this; it would look amazing
the general dictated to his aide,
a goat who smoked cigars.

I was an aristocratic detective

I was an aristocratic detective
known for baroque solutions
to seemingly insipid murders,

set-piece monologues
I diagramed using billiard tables,
croquet greens, fox hunts,
or whatever else was close at hand

in those quiet mansions
where everyone knew everything.

You were the well-aliased confidant
of many a dead thespian
whose demises corresponded
with their most timeless roles.

I questioned you gently,
monocle glistening
as your eyes signed RSVPs
against my graying body.

Wiping your lipstick
into an evidence bag,
I spoke of how even poison
could be an accessory,

but really all I kept thinking
was how very remarkable it is
that croquet fans are called Tragics

as the opera house unwound around us,
opulent and empty.

I was a traditional convict

I was a traditional convict,
my beard old-south gracious
and my hair so repentant
it fell out,

dusting a casual trail behind me
in case my movements
should ever be questioned again.

The great husky trains of America
set time tables for the superstitious,

stretching freight down-county
until their heavy light
shone across the prison walls,

a heavenly divination
suggestive in its lack of proscribed action.

The vibrations folded each night
into a machined rhythm,
a popular song.

Guitars quickened to shovels
within my stomach,
that well-known home
of a dozen abandoned tunnels.

I was a builder of champions

I was a builder of champions,
my muscles proselytizing dynamite
and new architectural definitions for symmetry
based on tiger strength

to the open admiration of all women,
nations of them trembling
as I showcased my magnificent appendages.

Friends, I once knew bully sand
with such an intimacy
that barnacles grew about my lips.

So skinny I was ashamed to strip,
I drew blindfolds
over my own pin-ups.

My physical measurements
were placed in a time capsule
and buried for posterity
underneath a forest.

Each winter, the trees flexed their ventricles
through the varsity wind,

stuck with nothing left to lose
but their own weakness.

I was encased in a block of ice

I was encased in a block of ice
for half-an-hour,
and I was thinking about you
the whole time,

the world growing slow and theoretical
until my blood stopped weaving tinsel
from the diagonal light.

The Newspaper Men's Midnight Frolic
was dense with thrill shows.

Rodeo stunt hoots
filled the aisles in peanut shells.

Portland screamed beside me
as the engineers leapt to safety,
their locomotives crashing together
to grow the promised debris of spectacle.

As if quoting the sentiments
clouded inside a diamond,
by the time my assistant broke me free,
I was speechless
and intensely calm.

I kept on melting
and the crowd cheered me on.

I was a drift of wrecked sailors

I was a drift of wrecked sailors
lost in the doldrums of
a loveless tropic,

a candlelight best described as dusk
patting down squalls
and folding the wind into blankets.

There was no rescue
washed in upon the tide,
only green and salty wigs
that broke against the beach

as the wind kept repeating
its constant, obnoxious message
to grow wings.

We lost any concept of blue
searching for a proper wink
inside the molding postcards that are the sea.

We holstered knots,
crossed fingers outlining anchors
through thin sheets.

We drew pictures of imaginary lovers,
each one smaller than the last.

I was a revolutionary artist

I was a revolutionary artist
after the revolution,
when workers paraded
under large representations of themselves

and the years eroded
into mundane slogans,

tobacco brands renamed
State Loan or *Industrialization.*

Windows seemed the sole medium
that could transcend the symbolism
of who we'd been, so I painted them,

my brush a primitive device
all but meaningless
in its repetition of terrible clergymen,

ravens clawing the stacks
of broken-down trains.

The farms needed sympathy.
The world needed something
to make its workers laugh.

My technique was similar
to that of a drunk who, after drinking,
proceeds to eat his own glass.

I was two anarchist bullfighters

I was two anarchist bullfighters
and a white haired schoolmaster

vibrating soundlessly as sympathetic strings
inside the sudden annotations
of the Spanish dawn
that ends your biography.

I was also the firing squad
standing opposite,
that anonymous physiology
of rifles, sweat, and careless tobacco.

Everything was routine.

The mountains did nothing.
The clouds did nothing.
The birds didn't hold their breath.

A child ate oranges on a balcony.
The bulls slept soundlessly.

Even the graves were wordless
in the implementation of their orders.

I was a forger's apprentice

I was a forger's apprentice
memorizing the ways ink bleeds
in evening light,

the stars full of signatures,
the moon a fingerprint
someone forgot to wipe.

I traced new stories
from our landscape's autographs:

the elegant apologies bent through rivers,
the constant exclamations of a cactus.

I even copied a farm
from some local seeds and an almanac.

Finally, I built a new me
and named it,
drinks bending the face to authenticity

while the hands were formal,
candlesticks, really
when they came to your body,

the bones hollow just in case.

I was a wartime censor

I was a wartime censor
seeding letters with sudden shadows
like visual static,

a hundred possible sentences
aging the vague, contagious darkness.

Where there had been cities,
I left islands.

I worked in complete silence.
Our blockade's machinery
had been undertaken
on a scale so unprecedented

that curtains of fog
surrounded my desk

as if mirroring the distant, storm-beaten ships
I kept trying to protect.

A quiet jubilation
consumed my rejoicing hands
in something like affection

whenever I found a metaphor
overlooked by my platoon.

Chess moves to coordinates off the table.
Postcards that read only
I believe you owe me a letter.

I was a lonely heiress

I was a lonely heiress
born to a dynasty so traditional
our mansion's windowless-ness
only seemed sensible,

a pathologically confidential architecture
concealing roomfuls
of well-polished shackles
where matrons ate manicured sandwiches.

It was a terrifying life
until all my relations died.

I walked outside and hired a carpenter
to construct dollhouses
full of murder scenes.

I enlarged the sky
to create a more intricate problem.

Wallpaper stood in for fingerprints
in those tiny rooms,
where everything was psychological.

Policemen renamed me
the Patron Saint of Evidence,

the mother of a new forensics
dependent on each inspector
imagining themselves six inches tall.

I was an airborne crew

I was an airborne crew
when sometimes distant cities
were only fire

and sometimes there were no cities at all
to explain the sky at night,

latticework tracing the stars
into birds who, once folded, flew.

Like intelligence concerning the topical weather
our bodies became,
arrows covered flight-maps

and the real moon cried,
a diagram each night
graphing our chances of survival.

Off-duty, we drank gravitas.
We smoked two cigarettes at once
in the hopes of looking older.
We rubbed our eyes.

The mess-hall exploded
in a brave, loud din

as something inside us
broke off ghosts from the terror
we wore like uniforms.

I was a professional spy

I was a professional spy
when distinguished scars
were the only fingerprints you could depend on

and some trees weren't trees
so much as telegrams
sent by my predecessors,
the stupid missionaries.

You could order a revolver
through room service
or check an alibi by cutting off your own arm,
those days.

You could say goodbye
and really mean it.

Mostly, I spied on people
by watching what they were doing.

Sometimes I imagined you
a distant historian
combing through hotel registers
to trace my aliases,

like you might know my face
from only this awful handwriting
of who I was today.

I was a flea tamer

I was a flea tamer
presenting historical reenactments
of opulent coronations
and famous assassinations.

My hat was a folded newspaper.

My milky-white arm
was the patron saint of fleas.
No honorable man could stand me.

Wallpaper peeled away
from my smoke-painted showroom
like a quiet hustle

and John Wilkes Flea did his thing again,
aiming an eyelash rifle
from a neon-lit cardboard balcony.

A Siberian exile taught me
what he learned in seven years
chained to a salt-mine wheelbarrow.

That the sky can shrink,
a glass box that teaches fleas not to jump.

That anything is obscene
if you stare close enough.

I was ghostmaster

I was ghostmaster,
my whiskers barbered
to poster lightning

as the spook-show rolled
its fantastic congress of horrors
through a thousand nickel-house midnights.

Black River or Mercy Hat
held themselves against the emptiness
whispered against rural maps

as if our route were recreating
the frightening travelogues
of those pilgrims
who tried to settle their own shadows.

In the morning
I checked my body for memories
but found only stage makeup,
a smudged gloaming.

On the dash, wax fangs melted
to blank fingerprints
as sunlight shot detectives
through the trailer slats.

I was an alcoholic mascot

I was an alcoholic mascot,
a crepuscular aristocrat
fiendishly done up in spats, a gold vest,

and a jolly silhouette
that left nothing but religious questions
to the imagination.

Old sailing captains often lashed a keg of whiskey
under their rocking chairs,

the company paid me to say
and repeat indefinitely.

The decades clothed me
in slight variations:
monocle, pince-nez, opera glasses.

Such was my leisure as to always be drinking,
my jeweled cane skittering
its vaguely fascist scrip
from New Bedford all the way to Albany.

Enthusiasm tore volcanoes through my veins.
I sold an idea of a feeling.

Then I sold it harder.

I was a stage magician

I was a stage magician
patenting flawed illusions
to confuse imitators
and all you students of the future,

who could deduce only
that I was a horrible primary source
in a sharpened tuxedo.

Onstage, I proceeded
straight to the comic decapitations
and bullet switches.

Eating live munitions,
I breathed fireworks indiscriminately,
my tongue a black tourniquet.

Theatre-grade lightning
played over the audience
and I thought about fainting,
what a curtain it is

when our hearts flutter,
flags in a gentle wind.

I spit out my assistant.
Another show was about to begin.

I was the legendary singing moose of Calgary

I was the legendary singing moose of Calgary
until my baritone rusted into a simple call
bereft of popular significance

and my employer found a blue-jay
named The Wizard of The North
proficient in Christmas favorites.

There was a meadow I used as backstage.
It smelled of postcards
so I closed my eyes and rambled there,

my antlers deflating
into forlorn glaciers.

No mere humming, my bass emoted
a majestic kingdom of ideal timber.

The bar went silent,
walls lined in my ancestors
caught in deep, lonesome echoes.

Glass tears filled glass eyes.
The peanuts weren't really endless.

I was an auctioneering champion

I was an auctioneering champion
peppering my chants with Old Testament chestnuts
and patent nonsense,

my tongue preaching commerce
through its raw, assonant mathematics

as a hundred rich Texans
hunched breathless in the bleachers.

Deep inside the heart of agriculture,
there was a semaphore.

It took the form of slight nods,
quickly scratched chins.

The auction became a living thing,
a rhythmic ghost raised high
upon its quiet bidding.

What love I had
for whoever placed telephone poles
along our nation's highways!

That I could imagine voices
traveling faster than my own,

yours among them only
as beautiful as the landscape,
emptied as it was
of everything that could be sold.

I was a handsome privateer

I was a handsome privateer
the critics dismissed
as born centuries too late,

airplanes painting quotation marks
across the horizon

as margaritas defeated scurvy
and I invaded
the Tropic of Capricorn.

Chains, squeeze-box and staggering
clothed a chorus I heard
when I couldn't sleep.

The gentle weeping
some men called a furious sea
invested locally in me.

Each block was an amnesty garden,
a storybook Africa,
an island in solidarity with all islands.

I walked them furiously,
rusty hooks and peg-legs
blooming intermittently

like exclamations or question marks
whose answers only I knew.

I was a second-tier airport chaplain

I was a second-tier airport chaplain
stuck in terminal L for Love,
a skyward place
of thick, federal gravity

where I collected the confessions
of pilots who had fallen in love
with continental breakfasts.

Wifeless on the tarmac,
spent pin-ups of darkness
brightened into 1983.

The night was full of thunder
and my mouth was a fireworks
blessing everything.

My collar felt plastic, a snap-on wing.

Yes, I thought about sea captains:
how they can marry any couple for a week

and what a marriage that would be,
its end visible from the quarterdeck,
larger every day,

every room a distant shore,
every night a runway.

I was a home for old soldiers

I was a home for old soldiers
to smoke away wounds
and try to remember Irkutsk
or whatever else had been classified by aging.

The bedrooms between wars, maybe,
boudoirs plastered in ticker-tape.

For the cemetery behind me,
the only parade was the weather,
which was terrible.

It stood clumsy,
a hundred teeth bumping against each other
to appear as just one storm.

By November, the trees revealed dictations
correspondent to the current war
so I kept a room empty for you, my friend,

each line of cracked paint
graphing a pirate's lullaby, I mean a sinking
arranged for solo trumpet,

I mean your eye
magnified through a rifle sight.

I was a cliff-side lookout

I was a cliff-side lookout
built for a soldiery discontinued
by modern warfare,

a stiff-lip satellite all cement and waiting
through years that smoked themselves

and endless lungs
for flotillas that never came.

The possibility of battles
saved my attendant, wooded acres from retirees.

Their silhouettes, I mean,
plaques summarizing what might have been

like company towns
as views became lecterns

Every day suggested
the end of the world
unencumbered by any fortifications
other than the sea,

the light accidentally keeping time
like trees,

the lovely drunk children
the bluffs eroded around me.

I was a performing bear impersonator

I was a performing bear impersonator
specializing in blindfolded motorcycle stunts
for corporate parades
and contingency Super Bowls.

During our first date,
I licked my own skin habitually.

We ate tacos.

Like the slowest dancing
a cowboy might imagine
after months of wrangling shadows,

simply breathing
outside the animatronics I wore
completely destroyed me.

Nightly, my musk was reborn.

To be faithful to the original sadness
capture brings,

tricks that seemed stressful and confusing
when attempted by real bears
became acts of redemption
in commercial form.

I stood on white sand.
You wore a bikini.
True wilderness washed ashore.

I was a modernist cemetery

I was a modernist cemetery
whose monuments were loved more

than the men and women they followed,
well-dressed in silence
and everything else inherent to death's form:

posthumous manicures,
feeling like you're made of sticks,
a rigid sense of order.

Rather than epitaphs,
each headstone was chiseled in ellipses
to omit what couldn't be understood,

an absence made formal by rain
and critics.

The sky might well have been English.

Underneath their leaves,
the trees wore rivers of such generic cut
the earth seemed modest,

its metaphors obvious as obelisks
or a remix's "fifth wall."

Bereft of everything but ritual,
my pretensions eroded:
Infinite Owls

I was a bankrupt circus

I was a bankrupt circus
burning stage clouds for puppet meat

as mandrakes blurred
and day broke, a velvet throat
suddenly auctioning off the periphery.

Newly minted ephemera surrounded us
like a party-size abracadabra.

Mountains broke the panorama
into a parable about false teeth,
a telegram that only read *stop*.

It only rained under our umbrellas.

Morning light made clowns of everything,
elephants wilting to paper-mache.

Through the flames, our itinerary crumpled
into a panhandle of vacant townships,
prune ribbons of torn river.

What dreams we wanted to seem
slowly burned away.

I was a county fairground

I was a county fairground
feathered under winter's soft, physical salute,

a fine topography
smoldering derby turf dutifully
the way settlers explained memory
to their wretched crops.

A tree bisected the spangled bones
of my Ferris Wheel.

The midway guessed its own weight.

Empty, my bleachers became tributes
to the utopian bias
absence deputizes upon just about anything.

Like a magician's pivotal moment
when he takes off his mustache
and uses it as a dagger
to rescue children from the devil,

you, the year's first vandal,
found me
memorized by the rust.

You saved me
by slowly repeating your own name.

I was an invisible man

I was an invisible man
muttering the conspiracies to sleep
in smoke-stained monotone
when you couldn't,

transmissions unwinding the distance
between Nevada and tomorrow

through the thick, cordoned hours.

My words echoed slightly,
dusting their own shadows
for evidence.

I interviewed spoon-benders,
slow-voiced hypnotists,
and farmers who'd seen holes so deep
they'd bring your dogs back to life.

Our borders expanded at night.

So did my voice,
faceless as I spoke
ghosts down to Texas.

Coast to coast,
a congress of small lit rooms
knit an earthly constellation
inside the darkness.

Thanks to the editors of the following journals in which these poems first appeared:
The Australian Book Review, Bird Dog, The Concher, Conjunctions, English, Field, Handsome, The Hat, The Hollins Critic, Lit Mag, Make, Mrs. Maybe, Ninth Letter, Parthenon West, Poetry London, Quarterly West, The Rialto, Ryga, Skein, Stand, Structo, Tuesday, Typo, West Branch.